SACREDSPACE

27 NOVEMBER 2022 TO 7 JANUARY 2023

FROM THE WEBSITE WWW.SACREDSPACE.IE
PRAYER FROM THE IRISH JESUITS

Designed by Messenger Publications Design Department
Typeset in Adobe Caslon Pro & ITC Avant Garde
Cover Image: Copyright © Andrda/Shutterstock.
Printed by GPS Colour Graphics

Messenger Publications,
37 Leeson Place, Dublin D02 E5V0, Ireland
www.messenger.ie

CONTENTS

Sacred Space Prayer

Bless all who worship you, almighty God,
from the rising of the sun to its setting:
from your goodness enrich us,
by your love inspire us,
by your Spirit guide us,
by your power protect us,
in your mercy receive us,
now and always.

How to Use This Book

During each week of Advent, begin by reading the 'Something to think and pray about each day this week'. Then go through 'the Presence of God', 'Freedom' and 'Consciousness' steps to help you prepare yourself to hear the Word of God speaking to you. In the next step, 'The Word', turn to the Scripture reading for each day of the week. Inspiration points are provided if you need them. Then return to the 'conversation' and 'conclusion' steps. Follow this process every day of Advent.

The Advent retreat at the back of this book follows a similar structure: an invitation to experience stillness, a Scripture passage and reflection points, and suggestions for prayer; you may find it useful to move back and forth between the daily reflections and the retreat.

27 November–3 December 2022

Something to think and pray about each day this week:

Advent is a time when, as a Church, we journey together and realise our need for the Lord to save us. It is the same plea of the disciples to a sleeping Jesus on the storm-torn Sea of Galilee: 'Save us, Lord, we are going down' (Matthew 8:25). We all have our personal storms, where we tend to feel God is asleep in the middle of the messiness and mayhem of our lives. Our Church has been navigating a seemingly endless journey through choppy waters.

Advent enables us to see the present world as a signpost to a larger reality. Advent gives us a glimpse of hope amidst the ruins in our lives. Advent anticipates and waits for Christ's return, who pledges a solemn promise to free us from all that corrupts and defaces our personal and collective lives.

John Cullen,
Alert, Aware Attentive: Advent Reflections

The Presence of God

'Be still, and know that I am God.' Lord, your words lead us to the calmness and greatness of your presence.

Freedom

I am free. When I look at these words in writing, they seem to create in me a feeling of awe. Yes, a wonderful feeling of freedom. Thank you, God.

Consciousness

At this moment, Lord, I turn my thoughts to you.
I will leave aside my chores and preoccupations.
I will take rest and refreshment in your presence, Lord.

The Word

The word of God comes down to us through the Scriptures. May the Holy Spirit enlighten my mind and my heart to respond to the Gospel teachings.
(Please turn to the Scripture on the following pages. Inspiration points are there, should you need them. When you are ready, return here to continue.)

Conversation

Begin to talk with Jesus about the Scripture you have just read. What part of it strikes a chord in you? Perhaps the words of a friend – or some story you have heard recently – will slowly rise to the surface of your consciousness. If so, does the story throw light on what the Scripture passage may be trying to say to you?

Conclusion

Glory be to the Father, and to the Son, and to the
    Holy Spirit,
As it was in the beginning, is now and ever shall be,
World without end. Amen.

Sunday 27 November
First Sunday of Advent
Matthew 24:37–44

Jesus said, For as the days of Noah were, so will be the coming of the Son of Man. For as in those days before the flood they were eating and drinking, marrying and giving in marriage, until the day Noah entered the ark, and they knew nothing until the flood came and swept them all away, so too will be the coming of the Son of Man. Then two will be in the field; one will be taken and one will be left Two women will be grinding meal together; one will be taken and one will be left. Keep awake therefore, for you do not know on what day your Lord is coming. But understand this: if the owner of the house had known in what part of the night the thief was coming, he would have stayed awake and would not have let his house be broken into. Therefore you also must be ready, for the Son of Man is coming at an unexpected hour.'

- Jesus is not asking us to stay awake all night, but to live in the present, so that we can recognise the Lord when he appears in our lives. He shows himself in the unrehearsed moments, the interruptions and accidents that can throw us off balance.
- Teach me, Lord, to recognise your face wherever I encounter you.

Monday 28 November
Matthew 8:5–11

When he entered Capernaum, a centurion came to him, appealing to him and saying, 'Lord, my servant is lying at home paralysed, in terrible distress.' And he said to him, 'I will come and cure him.' The centurion answered, 'Lord, I am not worthy to have you come under my roof; but only speak the word, and my servant will be healed. For I also am a man under authority, with soldiers under me; and I say to one, "Go", and he goes, and to another, "Come", and he comes, and to my slave, "Do this", and the slave does it.' When Jesus heard him, he was amazed and said to those who followed him, 'Truly I tell you, in no one in Israel have I found such faith. I tell you, many will come from east and west and will eat with Abraham and Isaac and Jacob in the kingdom of heaven.'

- The centurion interceded with Jesus on behalf of his servant, not himself. Who do I want to intercede for today?

- 'Lord, I am not worthy.' Do I ever feel that way? Do I ever feel I am getting more than I deserve? We live in a culture of entitlement, thinking we deserve to get everything on offer. How about me?

Tuesday 29 November
Luke 10:21–24

At that same hour Jesus rejoiced in the Holy Spirit and said, 'I thank you, Father, Lord of heaven and earth, because you have hidden these things from the wise and the intelligent and have revealed them to infants; yes, Father, for such was your gracious will. All things have been handed over to me by my Father; and no one knows who the Son is except the Father, or who the Father is except the Son and anyone to whom the Son chooses to reveal him.'

Then, turning to the disciples, Jesus said to them privately, 'Blessed are the eyes that see what you see! For I tell you that many prophets and kings desired to see what you see, but did not see it, and to hear what you hear, but did not hear it.'

- Gratitude was important in Jesus' life as he rejoiced in the Holy Spirit and gave thanks to the Father. Giving thanks is important in the lives of all who follow Jesus for all we have is gift (1 Corinthians 4:7). It is the humble who can receive and acknowledge gifts and be grateful. The self-sufficient are not open to it, as they do not experience the need of what Jesus offers.
- We need freedom to receive gifts as we often think we have to earn them or justify them. The invitation is to live the truth of who we are and who God is for us. During this time of prayer, what am I grateful for?

Wednesday 30 November
St Andrew, Apostle
Matthew 4:18–22

As he walked by the Sea of Galilee, he saw two brothers, Simon, who is called Peter, and Andrew his brother, casting a net into the lake – for they were fishermen. And he said to them, 'Follow me, and I will make you fish for people.' Immediately they left their nets and followed him. As he went from there, he saw two other brothers, James son of Zebedee and his brother John, in the boat with their father Zebedee, mending their nets, and he called them. Immediately they left the boat and their father, and followed him.

- 'Immediately they left their nets and followed him.' What an example is set for us by Peter, Andrew, James and John! There is no 'shortly', 'maybe tomorrow', 'I'm busy just now'.
- What nets do I need to leave in order to follow Jesus wholeheartedly? What obstacles, what material attachments, what comfort zones have wound themselves so tightly around me that I cannot get up and follow him?

Thursday 1 December
Matthew 7:21.24–27

'Not everyone who says to me, "Lord, Lord", will enter the kingdom of heaven, but only one who does the will of my Father in heaven.

'Everyone then who hears these words of mine and acts on them will be like a wise man who built his house on rock. The rain fell, the floods came, and the winds blew and beat on that house, but it did not fall, because it had been founded on rock. And everyone who hears these words of mine and does not act on them will be like a foolish man who built his house on sand. The rain fell, and the floods came, and the winds blew and beat against that house, and it fell – and great was its fall!'

- We all know that actions speak louder than words. We are told here that our eternal life depends upon our ability to act according to God's will. It is a stark message, but it is reassuring to know that our true efforts will reap their own rewards.
- I am challenged by Jesus to take time daily to reflect and discern the Father's will. Otherwise I will live a shallow life that will not survive the floods and storms of life.

Friday 2 December
Matthew 9:27–31

As Jesus went on from there, two blind men followed him, crying loudly, 'Have mercy on us, Son of David!' When he entered the house, the blind men came to him; and Jesus said to them, 'Do you believe that I am able to do this?' They said to him, 'Yes, Lord.' Then he touched their eyes and said, 'According to your faith let it be done to you.' And their eyes were opened. Then Jesus sternly ordered them, 'See that no one knows of this.' But they went away and spread the news about him throughout that district.

- Desire is important in life. I am guided by knowing what I want, and having energy to pursue it. The Lord has desires for me too. These desires can meet, as happened for the blind men. Their faith and their need brought them to Jesus. I am invited to do the same, recognising that Jesus can transform my desires to bring them into harmony with his own.
- What are my deepest desires and how influential are they in living as a follower of Jesus? I pray to be in touch with Jesus' desire for me, knowing that my blindness can get in the way.

Saturday 3 December
Matthew 9:35; 10:1.5a.6–8

Then Jesus went about all the cities and villages, teaching in their synagogues, and proclaiming the good news of the kingdom, and curing every disease and every sickness.

Then Jesus summoned his twelve disciples and gave them authority over unclean spirits, to cast them out, and to cure every disease and every sickness.

These twelve Jesus sent out with the following instructions: 'Go nowhere among the Gentiles, and enter no town of the Samaritans, but go rather to the lost sheep of the house of Israel. As you go, proclaim the good news, "The kingdom of heaven has come near." Cure the sick, raise the dead, cleanse the lepers, cast out demons. You received without payment; give without payment.'

- Do I know any people who are harassed and helpless like sheep without a shepherd? Let me hold them before my mind's eye for a moment. Can I now imagine Jesus looking at them? How does he see them?

- If I feel harassed and helpless, how does he see me? I ask for the grace to look on the world around me with the compassionate eyes of Jesus

The Second Week of Advent

4–10 December 2022

Something to think and pray about each day this week:

It is possible to live a merely sentient existence, paying attention only to the immediate and being satisfied once the urgent, obvious appetites are met. It is hard to say how many manage to sustain this form of sleepwalking! In our better moments, we all know that this is wholly inadequate, even on a merely human level. We are all of us called to rise above mere existence and to live life abundantly (cf. John 10:10). In the faith, the Advent call is to wake up from our slumbers. *Metanoia* (conversion or repentance) means a whole change of mindset, going right down to the roots of our being. It's the only game in town. Of course it takes time, but the time is *now*.

Kieran J. O'Mahony OSA,
Hearers of the Word: Praying and Exploring the
Readings for Advent and Christmas

The Presence of God

'Come to me, all you who are weary and are carrying heavy burdens, and I will give you rest.' Here I am, Lord. I come to seek your presence. I long for your healing power.

Freedom

'In these days, God taught me as a schoolteacher teaches a pupil' (St Ignatius).

I remind myself that there are things God has to teach me yet, and I ask for the grace to hear those things and let them change me.

Consciousness

Help me, Lord, to be more conscious of your presence. Teach me to recognise your presence in others.

Fill my heart with gratitude for the times your love has been shown to me through the care of others.

The Word

God speaks to each of us individually. I listen attentively to hear what he is saying to me. Read the text a few times, then listen.

(Please turn to the Scripture on the following pages. Inspiration points are there, should you need them. When you are ready, return here to continue.)

Conversation

Conversation requires talking and listening.

As I talk to Jesus, may I also learn to be still and listen.

I picture the gentleness in his eyes and the smile full of love as he gazes on me.

I can be totally honest with Jesus as I tell him of my worries and my cares.

I will open my heart to him as I tell him of my fears and my doubts.

I will ask him to help me place myself fully in his care and to abandon myself to him, knowing that he always wants what is best for me.

Conclusion

I thank God for these moments we have spent together and for any insights I have been given concerning the text.

Sunday 4 December
Second Sunday of Advent
Matthew 3:1–12

In those days John the Baptist appeared in the wilderness of Judea, proclaiming, 'Repent, for the kingdom of heaven has come near.' This is the one of whom the prophet Isaiah spoke when he said,

'The voice of one crying out in the wilderness:
"Prepare the way of the Lord,
make his paths straight."'

Now John wore clothing of camel's hair with a leather belt around his waist, and his food was locusts and wild honey. Then the people of Jerusalem and all Judea were going out to him, and all the region along the Jordan, and they were baptised by him in the river Jordan, confessing their sins.

But when he saw many Pharisees and Sadducees coming for baptism, he said to them, 'You brood of vipers! Who warned you to flee from the wrath to come? Bear fruit worthy of repentance. Do not presume to say to yourselves, "We have Abraham as our ancestor"; for I tell you, God is able from these stones to raise up children to Abraham. Even now the axe is lying at the root of the trees; every tree therefore that does not bear good fruit is cut down and thrown into the fire.

'I baptise you with water for repentance, but one who is more powerful than I is coming after me; I am not worthy to carry his sandals. He will baptise you with the Holy Spirit and fire. His winnowing-fork is in his hand, and he will clear his threshing-floor and will gather his wheat into the granary; but the chaff he will burn with unquenchable fire.'

- I may feel uncomfortable when confronted with John's call to repentance, but I let myself listen, acknowledging that I am a sinner in need of God's mercy. If I cannot admit this, Advent is not for me.

Monday 5 December
Luke 5:17–26

One day, while he was teaching, Pharisees and teachers of the law were sitting nearby (they had come from every village of Galilee and Judea and from Jerusalem); and the power of the Lord was with him to heal. Just then some men came, carrying a paralysed man on a bed. They were trying to bring him in and lay him before Jesus; but finding no way to bring him in because of the crowd, they went up on the roof and let him down with his bed through the tiles into the middle of the crowd in front of Jesus. When he saw their faith, he said, 'Friend, your sins are forgiven you.' Then the scribes and the Pharisees began to question, 'Who is this who is speaking blasphemies? Who can forgive sins but God alone?' When Jesus perceived their questionings, he answered them, 'Why do you raise such questions in your hearts? Which is easier, to say, "Your sins are forgiven you", or to say, "Stand up and walk"? But so that you may know that the Son of Man has authority on earth to forgive sins' – he said to the one who was paralysed – 'I say to you, stand up and take your bed and go to your home.' Immediately he stood up before them, took what he had been lying on, and went to his home, glorifying God. Amazement seized all of them, and they glorified God and were filled with awe, saying, 'We have seen strange things today.'

- The paralysed man would not have been able to get to Jesus without the help of his friends. We need help also. Can I think of anyone who needs a helping hand from me?

Tuesday 6 December
Matthew 18:12–14
Jesus said, 'What do you think? If a shepherd has a hundred sheep, and one of them has gone astray, does he not leave the ninety-nine on the mountains and go in search of the one that went astray? And if he finds it, truly I tell you, he rejoices over it more than over the ninety-nine that never went astray. So it is not the will of your Father in heaven that one of these little ones should be lost.'

- Do I believe in the value of one? If each Christian helped even one person at a time, the world would be changed. But do I sometimes ignore both the ninety-nine – and also the one?

- If it is God's desire that none of the 'little ones' should be lost, that must be the desire of my heart also. To what 'little one' can I reach out today?

Wednesday 7 December
Matthew 11:28–30
Jesus said, 'Come to me, all you that are weary and are carrying heavy burdens, and I will give you rest. Take my yoke upon you, and learn from me; for I am gentle and humble in heart, and you will find rest for your souls. For my yoke is easy, and my burden is light.'

- This simple invitation goes straight to the heart. I spend time letting it echo within me, as I bring to Jesus all my weariness and heavy burdens, one by one.
- 'Learn from me; for I am gentle and humble in heart.' One of the most popular titles for Jesus in the Gospel was that of Rabbi, teacher. Here he invites us to learn from him: he describes himself as gentle and humble. Were these the two qualities he liked most about himself, where he wants us to be most like him? I pray to be a good student of this unique teacher.

Thursday 8 December

The Immaculate Conception of the Blessed Virgin Mary
Luke 1:26–38

In the sixth month the angel Gabriel was sent by God to a town in Galilee called Nazareth, to a virgin engaged to a man whose name was Joseph, of the house of David. The virgin's name was Mary. And he came to her and said, 'Greetings, favoured one! The Lord is with you.' But she was much perplexed by his words and pondered what sort of greeting this might be. The angel said to her, 'Do not be afraid, Mary, for you have found favour with God. And now, you will conceive in your womb and bear a son, and you will name him Jesus. He will be great, and will be called the Son of the Most High, and the Lord God will give to him the throne of his ancestor David. He will reign over the house of Jacob for ever, and of his kingdom there will be no end.' Mary said to the angel, 'How can this be, since I am a virgin?' The angel said to her, 'The Holy Spirit will come upon you, and the power of the Most High will overshadow you; therefore the child to be born will be holy; he will be called Son of God. And now, your relative Elizabeth in her old age has also conceived a son; and this is the sixth month for her who was said to be barren. For nothing will be impossible with God.' Then Mary said, 'Here am I, the servant of the Lord; let it be with me according to your word.' Then the angel departed from her.

- Let us consider today that, long before we were born, we are called by God to know, love and serve him. We have been the constant recipients of his blessings. Do we notice these in our daily lives? Do we take time to listen to the still small voice of God in our day?

Friday 9 December
Matthew 11:16–19

Jesus said, 'But to what will I compare this generation? It is like children sitting in the market-places and calling to one another,

"We played the flute for you, and you did not dance;

we wailed, and you did not mourn."

For John came neither eating nor drinking, and they say, "He has a demon"; the Son of Man came eating and drinking, and they say, "Look, a glutton and a drunkard, a friend of tax-collectors and sinners!" Yet wisdom is vindicated by her deeds.'

- We live in a world with many prejudices. The person who says something can be taken as more important than what was said. There can be failure to acknowledge the context. While Jesus' life-style was very different from that of John, both were rejected. The hearers saw the difficulty as outside themselves, not within. They needed wisdom to be able to interpret the truth of the call to change.

• The Lord desires me to be free. I have my own prejudices. Where am I called to be more free of them? Who are the tax collectors and sinners that I am called to befriend? I ask the Lord for the freedom that opens me more fully to follow him more closely.

Saturday 10 December
Matthew 17:9a.10–13

As they were coming down the mountain, Jesus ordered them, 'Tell no one about the vision until after the Son of Man has been raised from the dead.' And the disciples asked him, 'Why, then, do the scribes say that Elijah must come first?' He replied, 'Elijah is indeed coming and will restore all things; but I tell you that Elijah has already come, and they did not recognise him, but they did to him whatever they pleased. So also the Son of Man is about to suffer at their hands.' Then the disciples understood that he was speaking to them about John the Baptist.

• The desire for signs is a common experience. Elijah had been taken up in a whirlwind, so there was a belief that he would come again. John the Baptist was similar to Elijah in many ways – another fiery prophet. John was carrying the role of Elijah. Both suffered because of their teaching. Jesus as a prophet would face the same reality.

• There is a call to recognise who is truly prophetic

and have the courage and conviction to follow that. How do I recognise false prophets at this time? I pray to be prophetic in living and sharing the Good News of Jesus' coming in our midst.

The Third Week of Advent

11–17 December 2022

Something to think and pray about each day this week:

Pope Francis says: 'There is no prayer in which Jesus does not inspire us to do something.' Our faith in Jesus is seen in strong action. The poor are helped at our pre-Christmas collections. We might ask not what we might get for Christmas, but how our Christmas might help others. We might ask that Christmas will be happy for others because of us happy in body, with enough food for every family, happy in mind that we know the truth of God's coming into the world, and happy in forgiveness, as that is one of God's biggest gifts.

Donal Neary SJ,
Gospel Reflections for Sundays of Year A

The Presence of God

'I am standing at the door, knocking,' says the Lord. What a wonderful privilege that the Lord of all creation desires to come to me. I welcome his presence.

Freedom

Leave me here freely all alone. / In cell where never sunlight shone. / Should no one ever speak to me. / This golden silence makes me free!
 – Part of a poem written by a prisoner at Dachau concentration camp

Consciousness

How am I really feeling? Lighthearted? Heavy-hearted? I may be very much at peace, happy to be here. Equally, I may be frustrated, worried or angry.
I acknowledge how I really am. It is the real me whom the Lord loves.

The Word

I take my time to read the word of God slowly, a few times, allowing myself to dwell on anything that strikes me.
(Please turn to the Scripture on the following pages. Inspiration points are there, should you need them. When you are ready, return here to continue.)

Conversation

Do I notice myself reacting as I pray with the word of God? Do I feel challenged, comforted, angry? Imagining Jesus sitting or standing by me, I speak out my feelings, as one trusted friend to another.

Conclusion

Glory be to the Father, and to the Son, and to the Holy Spirit,
As it was in the beginning, is now and ever shall be,
World without end. Amen.

Sunday 11 December
Third Sunday of Advent
Matthew 11:2–11

When John heard in prison what the Messiah was doing, he sent word by his disciples and said to him, 'Are you the one who is to come, or are we to wait for another?' Jesus answered them, 'Go and tell John what you hear and see: the blind receive their sight, the lame walk, the lepers are cleansed, the deaf hear, the dead are raised, and the poor have good news brought to them. And blessed is anyone who takes no offence at me.'

As they went away, Jesus began to speak to the crowds about John: 'What did you go out into the wilderness to look at? A reed shaken by the wind? What then did you go out to see? Someone dressed in soft robes? Look, those who wear soft robes are in royal palaces. What then did you go out to see? A prophet? Yes, I tell you, and more than a prophet. This is the one about whom it is written,

"See, I am sending my messenger ahead of you,
who will prepare your way before you."

'Truly I tell you, among those born of women no one has arisen greater than John the Baptist; yet the least in the kingdom of heaven is greater than he.'

- God's ways are not our ways. God is not predictable. We must be alert to 'the signs of the times' and accept the fact that God seems to live easily with change, and enjoys doing 'new things' (Isaiah 48:6).

Monday 12 December
Luke 1:26–38

In the sixth month the angel Gabriel was sent by God to a town in Galilee called Nazareth, to a virgin engaged to a man whose name was Joseph, of the house of David. The virgin's name was Mary. And he came to her and said, 'Greetings, favoured one! The Lord is with you.' But she was much perplexed by his words and pondered what sort of greeting this might be. The angel said to her, 'Do not be afraid, Mary, for you have found favour with God. And now, you will conceive in your womb and bear a son, and you will name him Jesus. He will be great, and will be called the Son of the Most High, and the Lord God will give to him the throne of his ancestor David. He will reign over the house of Jacob for ever, and of his kingdom there will be no end.' Mary said to the angel, 'How can this be, since I am a virgin?' The angel said to her, 'The Holy Spirit will come upon you, and the power of the Most High will overshadow you; therefore the child to be born will be holy; he will be called Son of God. And now, your relative Elizabeth in her old age has also conceived a son; and this is the sixth month for her who was said to be barren. For nothing will be impossible with God.' Then Mary said, 'Here am I, the servant of the Lord; let it be with me according to your word.' Then the angel departed from her.

• Lord, when the silence seems heavy and

impenetrable, I recall how it can be broken at the most unexpected times and in the most unexpected circumstances. Like Mary, I must be still enough to hear the voice and courageous enough to act on it.

Tuesday 13 December
Matthew 21:28–32

Jesus said to them, 'What do you think? A man had two sons; he went to the first and said, "Son, go and work in the vineyard today." He answered, "I will not"; but later he changed his mind and went. The father went to the second and said the same; and he answered, "I go, sir"; but he did not go. Which of the two did the will of his father?' They said, 'The first.' Jesus said to them, 'Truly I tell you, the tax-collectors and the prostitutes are going into the kingdom of God ahead of you. For John came to you in the way of righteousness and you did not believe him, but the tax-collectors and the prostitutes believed him; and even after you saw it, you did not change your minds and believe him.'

- This simple parable is turned into a fierce polemic against the chief priests and elders. This is understandable given their role in the Passion. Only in Luke's Gospel do we have the words of Jesus from the cross, 'Father forgive them, they know not what they do.' How would that fit into Matthew's Gospel?

Wednesday 14 December
Luke 7:18b–23

The disciples of John reported all these things to him. So John summoned two of his disciples and sent them to the Lord to ask, 'Are you the one who is to come, or are we to wait for another?' When the men had come to him, they said, 'John the Baptist has sent us to you to ask, "Are you the one who is to come, or are we to wait for another?"' Jesus had just then cured many people of diseases, plagues and evil spirits, and had given sight to many who were blind. And he answered them, 'Go and tell John what you have seen and heard: the blind receive their sight, the lame walk, the lepers are cleansed, the deaf hear, the dead are raised, the poor have good news brought to them. And blessed is anyone who takes no offence at me.'

• Lord, I can identify with John. I too find the wick of my lamp can quiver and splutter when things don't go my way. My desire for a world of peace and justice is met by a world of violence and injustice. This Advent day refill my inner lamp and let me walk in faith and trust.

Thursday 15 December
Luke 7:24–30

When John's messengers had gone, Jesus began to speak to the crowds about John: 'What did you go out into the wilderness to look at? A reed shaken by the wind? What then did you go out to see? Someone dressed in soft robes? Look, those who put on fine clothing and live in luxury are in royal palaces. What then did you go out to see? A prophet? Yes, I tell you, and more than a prophet. This is the one about whom it is written,

"See, I am sending my messenger ahead of you,
who will prepare your way before you."

'I tell you, among those born of women no one is greater than John; yet the least in the kingdom of God is greater than he.' (And all the people who heard this, including the tax-collectors, acknowledged the justice of God, because they had been baptised with John's baptism. But by refusing to be baptised by him, the Pharisees and the lawyers rejected God's purpose for themselves.)

• Jesus reminds the people of what they sought and found in John the Baptist: they did not search for some trivial reed or elegant courtesan but encountered a sign of God's presence. I take some time to recall and savour again the people who have helped me to discover God's ways.

Friday 16 December
John 5:33–36
Jesus said, 'You sent messengers to John, and he testified to the truth. Not that I accept such human testimony, but I say these things so that you may be

saved. He was a burning and shining lamp, and you were willing to rejoice for a while in his light. But I have a testimony greater than John's. The works that the Father has given me to complete, the very works that I am doing, testify on my behalf that the Father has sent me.'

- Jesus is clear about his mission – it comes from the Father. My mission is clear too: God wants me to live out of unconditional love. But do I want this mission? I talk with Jesus about this.

Saturday 17 December
Matthew 1:1–17

An account of the genealogy of Jesus the Messiah, the son of David, the son of Abraham.

Abraham was the father of Isaac, and Isaac the father of Jacob, and Jacob the father of Judah and his brothers, and Judah the father of Perez and Zerah by Tamar, and Perez the father of Hezron, and Hezron the father of Aram, and Aram the father of Aminadab, and Aminadab the father of Nahshon, and Nahshon the father of Salmon, and Salmon the father of Boaz by Rahab, and Boaz the father of Obed by Ruth, and Obed the father of Jesse, and Jesse the father of King David.

And David was the father of Solomon by the wife of Uriah, and Solomon the father of Rehoboam, and Rehoboam the father of Abijah, and Abijah the father of Asaph, and Asaph the father of Jehoshaphat, and Jehoshaphat the father of Joram, and Joram the father of Uzziah, and Uzziah the father of Jotham, and Jotham the father of Ahaz, and Ahaz the father of Hezekiah, and Hezekiah the father of Manasseh, and Manasseh the father of Amos, and Amos the father of Josiah, and Josiah the father of Jechoniah and his brothers, at the time of the deportation to Babylon.

And after the deportation to Babylon: Jechoniah was the father of Salathiel, and Salathiel the father of Zerubbabel, and Zerubbabel the father of Abiud, and Abiud the father of Eliakim, and Eliakim the father of Azor, and Azor the father of Zadok, and Zadok the father of Achim, and Achim the father of Eliud, and Eliud the father of Eleazar, and Eleazar the father of Matthan, and Matthan the father of Jacob, and Jacob the father of Joseph the husband of Mary, of whom Jesus was born, who is called the Messiah.

So all the generations from Abraham to David are fourteen generations; and from David to the deportation to Babylon, fourteen generations; and from the deportation to Babylon to the Messiah, fourteen generations.

• There are surprises in this list of Jesus' ancestors. Matthew's genealogy is revolutionary for his time, in that it features five women. In addition, four of the women were Gentiles. Add to that the presence of some notable sinners, like Judah and King David, and the intention is clear. It is to highlight the inclusivity of Jesus' mission.

The Fourth Week of Advent
18–24 December 2022

Something to think and pray about each day this week:

The text from a friend said that he wasn't sending Christmas cards but wanted to wish me peace and blessings at this special time. I called him back and asked if he was getting mean in his old age. I continued to joke with him for a little while and then he said, 'You mustn't have heard that my mother died.' I hadn't. He told me his mother had been diagnosed with cancer and died shortly after the diagnosis was given. I told him I'd not heard and of course he knew that because, had I heard, I'd have been there for him over those December days.

As we enter the final days of Advent, maybe we could remember him and how easy it is not to hear news. Gossip is all around us and seems to blow easily on the wind – easily and dangerously – but often the news we need to hear passes by unheard or untold. I wondered does God feel that way sometimes, not least around Christmas, and wondered how it is that this story, this very sacred story, can remain unheard and untold.

Vincent Sherlock, *Let Advent be Advent*

The Presence of God

'Be still, and know that I am God!' Lord, may your spirit guide me to seek your loving presence more and more for it is there I find rest and refreshment from this busy world.

Freedom

By God's grace I was born to live in freedom. Free to enjoy the pleasures he created for me. Dear Lord, grant that I may live as you intended, with complete confidence in your loving care.

Consciousness

How am I today?

Where am I with God? With others?

Do I have something to be grateful for? Then I give thanks.

Is there something I am sorry for? Then I ask forgiveness.

The Word

God speaks to each of us individually. I need to listen, to hear what he is saying to me. Read the text a few times, then listen.

(Please turn to the Scripture on the following pages. Inspiration points are there, should you need them. When you are ready, return here to continue.)

Conversation
How has God's word moved me? Has it left me cold?
Has it consoled me or moved me to act in a new way?
I imagine Jesus standing or sitting beside me.
I turn and share my feelings with him.

Conclusion
I thank God for these moments we have spent
together and for any insights I have been given
concerning the text.

Sunday 18 December
Fourth Sunday of Advent
Matthew 1:18–24

Now the birth of Jesus the Messiah took place in this way. When his mother Mary had been engaged to Joseph, but before they lived together, she was found to be with child from the Holy Spirit. Her husband Joseph, being a righteous man and unwilling to expose her to public disgrace, planned to dismiss her quietly. But just when he had resolved to do this, an angel of the Lord appeared to him in a dream and said, 'Joseph, son of David, do not be afraid to take Mary as your wife, for the child conceived in her is from the Holy Spirit. She will bear a son, and you are to name him Jesus, for he will save his people from their sins.' All this took place to fulfil what had been spoken by the Lord through the prophet·

'Look, the virgin shall conceive and bear a son,
    and they shall name him Emmanuel',

which means, 'God is with us.' When Joseph awoke from sleep, he did as the angel of the Lord commanded him; he took her as his wife.

- We are invited to take our challenging situations to the Lord in trust. God's surprising ways are revealed to Mary and to Joseph. Joseph, the righteous man, gives me a message on how to accept Jesus as Saviour. Lord, help me see the surprising ways in which you reveal yourself to me now.

Monday 19 December
Luke 1:5–25

In the days of King Herod of Judea, there was a priest named Zechariah, who belonged to the priestly order of Abijah. His wife was a descendant of Aaron, and her name was Elizabeth. Both of them were righteous before God, living blamelessly according to all the commandments and regulations of the Lord. But they had no children, because Elizabeth was barren, and both were getting on in years.

Once when he was serving as priest before God and his section was on duty, he was chosen by lot, according to the custom of the priesthood, to enter the sanctuary of the Lord and offer incense. Now at the time of the incense-offering, the whole assembly of the people was praying outside. Then there appeared to him an angel of the Lord, standing at the right side of the altar of incense. When Zechariah saw him, he was terrified; and fear overwhelmed him. But the angel said to him, 'Do not be afraid, Zechariah, for your prayer has been heard. Your wife Elizabeth will bear you a son, and you will name him John. You will have joy and gladness, and many will rejoice at his birth, for he will be great in the sight of the Lord. He must never drink wine or strong drink; even before his birth he will be filled with the Holy Spirit. He will turn many of the people of Israel to the Lord their God. With the spirit and power of Elijah he will go before him, to turn the hearts of parents to their children, and the disobedient to the wisdom of the righteous, to make ready a people prepared for the Lord.' Zechariah said to the angel, 'How will I know that this is so? For I am an old man, and my wife is getting on in years.' The angel replied, 'I am Gabriel. I stand in the presence of God, and I have been sent to speak to you and to bring you this good news. But now, because you did not believe my words, which will be fulfilled in their time, you will become mute, unable to speak, until the day these things occur.'

Meanwhile, the people were waiting for Zechariah, and wondered at his delay in the sanctuary. When he did come out, he could not speak to them, and they realised that he had seen a vision in the sanctuary. He kept motioning to them and remained unable to speak. When his time of service was ended, he went to his home.

After those days his wife Elizabeth conceived, and for five months she remained in seclusion. She said, 'This is what the Lord has done for me when he looked favourably on me and took away the disgrace I have endured among my people.'

- Zechariah and Elizabeth were not expecting these amazing things to happen to them; they were simply ordinary pious Jews living according to the Law. The things that happen in our lives are normally undramatic but just as much a part of God's plan.

Tuesday 20 December
Luke 1:26–38

In the sixth month the angel Gabriel was sent by God to a town in Galilee called Nazareth, to a virgin engaged to a man whose name was Joseph, of the house of David. The virgin's name was Mary. And he came to her and said, 'Greetings, favoured one! The Lord is with you.' But she was much perplexed by his words and pondered what sort of greeting this might be. The angel said to her, 'Do not be afraid, Mary, for you have found favour with God. And now, you will conceive in your womb and bear a son, and you will name him Jesus. He will be great, and will be called the Son of the Most High, and the Lord God will give to him the throne of his ancestor David. He will reign over the house of Jacob for ever, and of his kingdom there will be no end.' Mary said to the angel, 'How can this be, since I am a virgin?' The angel said to her, 'The Holy Spirit will come upon you, and the power of the Most High will overshadow you; therefore the child to be born will be holy; he will be called Son of God. And now, your relative Elizabeth in her old age has also conceived a son; and this is the sixth month for her who was said to be barren. For nothing will be impossible with God.' Then Mary said, 'Here am I, the servant of the Lord; let it be with me according to your word.' Then the angel departed from her.

• Nothing is impossible to God! In difficult times,

it is good to remember that God is fully in charge of our world. Everything happens according to his plan. There is always hope.

Wednesday 21 December
Luke 1:39–45

In those days Mary set out and went with haste to a Judean town in the hill country, where she entered the house of Zechariah and greeted Elizabeth. When Elizabeth heard Mary's greeting, the child leapt in her womb. And Elizabeth was filled with the Holy Spirit and exclaimed with a loud cry, 'Blessed are you among women, and blessed is the fruit of your womb. And why has this happened to me, that the mother of my Lord comes to me? For as soon as I heard the sound of your greeting, the child in my womb leapt for joy. And blessed is she who believed that there would be a fulfilment of what was spoken to her by the Lord.'

- Mary brought God to Elizabeth in her heart and in her womb. We bring God to everyone we meet, and everyone we meet brings God to us.

Thursday 22 December
Luke 1:46–56

And Mary said,

'My soul magnifies the Lord,
     and my spirit rejoices in God my Saviour,

for he has looked with favour on the lowliness of
   his servant.
 Surely, from now on all generations will call
   me blessed;
for the Mighty One has done great things for
   me,
 and holy is his name.
His mercy is for those who fear him
 from generation to generation.
He has shown strength with his arm;
 he has scattered the proud in the thoughts of
   their hearts.
He has brought down the powerful from their
   thrones,
 and lifted up the lowly;
he has filled the hungry with good things,
 and sent the rich away empty.
He has helped his servant Israel,
 in remembrance of his mercy,
according to the promise he made to our
   ancestors,
 to Abraham and to his descendants for ever.'
 And Mary remained with her for about three
months and then returned to her home.

• Mary prayed her own Magnificat. She is full
 of praise. Her grateful heart overflows with
 thanksgiving. God is the great one in her life,

working marvels beyond all imagining.

- Can I write my own Magnificat today? For what do I want to give thanks? Meister Eckhart wrote, 'If the only prayer we ever say is thanks, that will suffice.'

Friday 23 December
Luke 1:57–66

Now the time came for Elizabeth to give birth, and she bore a son. Her neighbours and relatives heard that the Lord had shown his great mercy to her, and they rejoiced with her.

On the eighth day they came to circumcise the child, and they were going to name him Zechariah after his father. But his mother said, 'No; he is to be called John.' They said to her, 'None of your relatives has this name.' Then they began motioning to his father to find out what name he wanted to give him. He asked for a writing-tablet and wrote, 'His name is John.' And all of them were amazed. Immediately his mouth was opened and his tongue freed, and he began to speak, praising God. Fear came over all their neighbours, and all these things were talked about throughout the entire hill country of Judea. All who heard them pondered them and said, 'What then will this child become?' For, indeed, the hand of the Lord was with him.

- Lord, praise, amazement and joy are hallmarks of a

life rooted in you. Fill me with these gifts. Enable me to be a tracer of your grace in my life and to lift up my voice in joyful thanksgiving.

Saturday 24 December
Luke 1:67–79

Then his father Zechariah was filled with the Holy Spirit and spoke this prophecy:

'Blessed be the Lord God of Israel,
   for he has looked favourably on his people and
      redeemed them.
He has raised up a mighty saviour for us
   in the house of his servant David,
as he spoke through the mouth of his holy
      prophets from of old,
   that we would be saved from our enemies and
      from the hand of all who hate us.
Thus he has shown the mercy promised to our
      ancestors,
   and has remembered his holy covenant,
the oath that he swore to our ancestor Abraham,
   to grant us that we, being rescued from the
      hands of our enemies,
might serve him without fear, in holiness and
      righteousness
   before him all our days.

And you, child, will be called the prophet of the
    Most High;
  for you will go before the Lord to prepare his
    ways,
to give knowledge of salvation to his people
  by the forgiveness of their sins.
By the tender mercy of our God,
  the dawn from on high will break upon us,
to give light to those who sit in darkness and in
    the shadow of death,
    to guide our feet into the way of peace.'

- God has come to rescue his people as he promised
long ago. The promise still holds for us. Whatever
trouble we may be in, God is coming to save us and
we can be at peace.

The First Week of Christmas

25–31 December 2022

Something to think and pray about each day this week:

Most homes have a crib of some sort; it is part of our Christmas. It brings the mystery of the birth of Jesus into our homes. Some church cribs have an open front – a sign that all are welcome. Many people feel unwelcome in the Church – people in second and other relationships that cause questions, people who have been through crime or in prison, people in addiction, families who feel the worse for what some family members have done, people of homosexual orientation, former priests and religious. Like the shepherds at the first crib, all are welcome. The Church welcomes all at this time of the year and, indeed, always. May we welcome all as God does, with the compassion and love of God?

Christmas reminds us to deal with each other in love and compassion. Someone was very harsh on someone when speaking to me recently. I just said, 'God loves him, and I would prefer to be with God on this one'. Just as we take a while to know the full story of Jesus, we take a while to know the full story of everyone.

Donal Neary SJ,
Gospel Reflections for Sundays of Year A

The Presence of God

As I sit here, the beating of my heart,
the ebb and flow of my breathing, the movements of
    my mind
are all signs of God's ongoing creation of me.
I pause for a moment and become aware
of this presence of God within me.

Freedom

Everything has the potential to draw from me a fuller
    love and life.
Yet my desires are often fixed, caught, on illusions of
    fulfilment.
I ask that God, through my freedom, may orchestrate
    my desires in a vibrant loving melody rich in
    harmony.

Consciousness

I ask, how am I within myself today? Am I
particularly tired, stressed or off-form? If any of these
characteristics apply, can I try to let go of the concerns
that disturb me?

The Word

I read the word of God slowly, a few times over, and I
listen to what God is saying to me.
*(Please turn to the Scripture on the following pages.
Inspiration points are there, should you need them. When you
are ready, return here to continue.)*

Conversation

I begin to talk with Jesus about the Scripture I have just read. What part of it strikes a chord in me? Perhaps the words of a friend or a story I have heard recently will slowly rise to the surface of my consciousness. If so, does the story throw light on what the Scripture passage may be trying to say to me?

Conclusion

Glory be to the Father, and to the Son, and to the Holy Spirit,
As it was in the beginning, is now and ever shall be,
World without end. Amen.

Sunday 25 December
The Nativity of the Lord
John 1:1–18

In the beginning was the Word, and the Word was with God, and the Word was God. He was in the beginning with God. All things came into being through him, and without him not one thing came into being. What has come into being in him was life, and the life was the light of all people. The light shines in the darkness, and the darkness did not overcome it.

There was a man sent from God, whose name was John. He came as a witness to testify to the light, so that all might believe through him. He himself was not the light, but he came to testify to the light. The true light, which enlightens everyone, was coming into the world.

He was in the world, and the world came into being through him; yet the world did not know him. He came to what was his own, and his own people did not accept him. But to all who received him, who believed in his name, he gave power to become children of God, who were born, not of blood or of the will of the flesh or of the will of man, but of God.

And the Word became flesh and lived among us, and we have seen his glory, the glory as of a father's only son, full of grace and truth. (John testified to him and cried out, 'This was he of whom I said, "He who comes after me ranks ahead of me because he was before me." ') From his fullness we have all received, grace upon grace. The law indeed was given through Moses; grace and truth came through Jesus Christ. No one has ever seen God. It is God the only Son, who is close to the Father's heart, who has made him known.

- Jesus is God's greatest gift to us. Prayer today can rest in the mystery of God, who is revealed to us in the coming of Jesus. From the beginning he was a sign to be rejected. Jesus desires to be at home with us and desires us to be at home with him. We pray to have room in our hearts and lives for him.

Monday 26 December
St Stephen, the First Martyr
Matthew 10:17–22
Jesus said to his disciples, 'Beware of them, for they will hand you over to councils and flog you in their synagogues; and you will be dragged before governors and kings because of me, as a testimony to them and the Gentiles. When they hand you over, do not worry about how you are to speak or what you are to say; for what you are to say will be given to you at that time; for it is not you who speak, but the Spirit of your Father speaking through you. Brother will betray brother to death, and a father his child, and children will rise against parents and have them put to death; and you will be hated by all because of my name. But

the one who endures to the end will be saved.'

- It can seem strange to celebrate St Stephen, who was martyred, right after Christmas Day when our dominant emotion is joy in the birth of Christ. The point, however, is that this is why Christ came on earth, to save us from our sins by his death on the Cross.

Tuesday 27 December
St John, Apostle and Evangelist
John 20:1a.2–8

Early on the first day of the week, while it was still dark, Mary Magdalene came to the tomb and saw that the stone had been removed from the tomb. So she ran and went to Simon Peter and the other disciple, the one whom Jesus loved, and said to them, 'They have taken the Lord out of the tomb, and we do not know where they have laid him.' Then Peter and the other disciple set out and went towards the tomb. The two were running together, but the other disciple outran Peter and reached the tomb first. He bent down to look in and saw the linen wrappings lying there, but he did not go in. Then Simon Peter came, following him, and went into the tomb. He saw the linen wrappings lying there, and the cloth that had been on Jesus' head, not lying with the linen wrappings but rolled up in a place by itself. Then the other disciple, who reached the tomb first, also went in, and he saw and believed.

- John saw and he believed. Blessed are those who have not seen and yet believe. That's us. Lord, help my unbelief.

Wednesday 28 December
Matthew 2:13–18

Now after they had left, an angel of the Lord appeared to Joseph in a dream and said, 'Get up, take the child and his mother, and flee to Egypt, and remain there until I tell you; for Herod is about to search for the child, to destroy him.' Then Joseph got up, took the child and his mother by night, and went to Egypt, and remained there until the death of Herod. This was to fulfil what had been spoken by the Lord through the prophet, 'Out of Egypt I have called my son.'

When Herod saw that he had been tricked by the wise men, he was infuriated, and he sent and killed all the children in and around Bethlehem who were two years old or under, according to the time that he had learned from the wise men. Then was fulfilled what had been spoken through the prophet Jeremiah:

'A voice was heard in Ramah,
   wailing and loud lamentation,
Rachel weeping for her children;
   she refused to be consoled, because they are no
      more.'

- The persecution of Christians for their faith

continues in our world today. Let us remember our brothers and sisters who are suffering and pray for them.

Thursday 29 December
Luke 2:22–35

When the time came for their purification according to the law of Moses, they brought him up to Jerusalem to present him to the Lord (as it is written in the law of the Lord, 'Every firstborn male shall be designated as holy to the Lord'), and they offered a sacrifice according to what is stated in the law of the Lord, 'a pair of turtle-doves or two young pigeons.'

Now there was a man in Jerusalem whose name was Simeon; this man was righteous and devout, looking forward to the consolation of Israel, and the Holy Spirit rested on him. It had been revealed to him by the Holy Spirit that he would not see death before he had seen the Lord's Messiah. Guided by the Spirit, Simeon came into the temple; and when the parents brought in the child Jesus, to do for him what was customary under the law, Simeon took him in his arms and praised God, saying,

> 'Master, now you are dismissing your servant in
>   peace,
>   according to your word;
> for my eyes have seen your salvation,

> which you have prepared in the presence of all
>   peoples,
> a light for revelation to the Gentiles
>   and for glory to your people Israel.'

And the child's father and mother were amazed at what was being said about him. Then Simeon blessed them and said to his mother Mary, 'This child is destined for the falling and the rising of many in Israel, and to be a sign that will be opposed so that the inner thoughts of many will be revealed – and a sword will pierce your own soul too.'

• Simeon recognised Jesus as 'a light for revelation to the Gentiles', and so for us. We in turn are to be a light for revelation to all those who have not yet accepted Jesus as the light of their lives.

Friday 30 December
The Holy Family of Jesus, Mary and Joseph
Matthew 2:13–15.19–23

Now after they had left, an angel of the Lord appeared to Joseph in a dream and said, 'Get up, take the child and his mother, and flee to Egypt, and remain there until I tell you; for Herod is about to search for the child, to destroy him.' Then Joseph got up, took the child and his mother by night, and went to Egypt, and remained there until the death of Herod. This was to fulfil what had been spoken by the Lord through the prophet, 'Out of Egypt I have called my son.'

When Herod died, an angel of the Lord suddenly appeared in a dream to Joseph in Egypt and said, 'Get up, take the child and his mother, and go to the land of Israel, for those who were seeking the child's life are dead.' Then Joseph got up, took the child and his mother, and went to the land of Israel. But when he heard that Archelaus was ruling over Judea in place of his father Herod, he was afraid to go there. And after being warned in a dream, he went away to the district of Galilee. There he made his home in a town called Nazareth, so that what had been spoken through the prophets might be fulfilled, 'He will be called a Nazorean.'

• The angels are delivering messages from God throughout the infancy narratives. We might think of our own guardian angel, whose role is 'to light, to guard, to rule and to guide' us.

Saturday 31 December
John 1:1–18

In the beginning was the Word, and the Word was with God, and the Word was God. He was in the beginning with God. All things came into being through him, and without him not one thing came into being. What has come into being in him was life, and the life was the light of all people. The light shines in the darkness, and the darkness did not overcome it.

There was a man sent from God, whose name was

John. He came as a witness to testify to the light, so that all might believe through him. He himself was not the light, but he came to testify to the light. The true light, which enlightens everyone, was coming into the world.

He was in the world, and the world came into being through him; yet the world did not know him. He came to what was his own, and his own people did not accept him. But to all who received him, who believed in his name, he gave power to become children of God, who were born, not of blood or of the will of the flesh or of the will of man, but of God.

And the Word became flesh and lived among us, and we have seen his glory, the glory as of a father's only son, full of grace and truth. (John testified to him and cried out, 'This was he of whom I said, "He who comes after me ranks ahead of me because he was before me." ') From his fullness we have all received, grace upon grace. The law indeed was given through Moses; grace and truth came through Jesus Christ. No one has ever seen God. It is God the only Son, who is close to the Father's heart, who has made him known.

- As our year draws to a close, today's scripture brings us back to the beginning of all time. As we stand on the threshold of another year, we take time to recall the greatest event of all: God has entered our world, not just for a day's visit, but has made it his permanent dwelling.

The Second Week of Christmas

1–7 January 2023

Something to think and pray about each day this week:

The beginning of a new year is an especially appropriate time to hear Jesus' question, 'What do you want?' as a question that is addressed to each of us personally. Jesus' second set of words in John's Gospel, again addressed to the disciples of John the Baptist, takes the form of an invitation, 'Come and see'. The question and the invitation very much go together. As we become aware of what it is we really want, we sense a call to set out on a journey towards the Lord as the one who alone can fully satisfy those deep hungers and thirsts in our hearts. The beginning of a new year is a good moment for us to get in touch with our deepest desire to see the Lord, and then to move closer to him, to grow in our relationship with him, so that we come to see and know him as he sees and knows us. We might allow both the question and the invitation of Jesus to resonate within us as we set out into the year that beckons.

Martin Hogan,
The Word of God is Living and Active

The Presence of God

Dear Jesus, I come to you today longing for your presence. I desire to love you as you love me. May nothing ever separate me from you.

Freedom

Lord, grant me the grace to be free from the excesses of this life. Let me not get caught up with the desire for wealth. Keep my heart and mind free to love and serve you.

Consciousness

Where do I sense hope, encouragement and growth in my life? By looking back over the past few months, I may be able to see which activities and occasions have produced rich fruit. If I do notice such areas, I will determine to give those areas both time and space in the future.

The Word

God speaks to each of us individually. I listen attentively to hear what he is saying to me. Read the text a few times, then listen.

(Please turn to the Scripture on the following pages. Inspiration points are there, should you need them. When you are ready, return here to continue.)

Conversation

What is stirring in me as I pray? Am I consoled,

troubled, left cold? I imagine Jesus standing or sitting at my side, and I share my feelings with him.

Conclusion

Glory be to the Father, and to the Son, and to the Holy Spirit,
As it was in the beginning, is now and ever shall be,
World without end. Amen.

Sunday 1 January
Mary, The Mother of God
Luke 2:16–21

So they went with haste and found Mary and Joseph, and the child lying in the manger. When they saw this, they made known what had been told them about this child; and all who heard it were amazed at what the shepherds told them. But Mary treasured all these words and pondered them in her heart. The shepherds returned, glorifying and praising God for all they had heard and seen, as it had been told them.

After eight days had passed, it was time to circumcise the child; and he was called Jesus, the name given by the angel before he was conceived in the womb.

- Mary had a unique relationship with the Blessed Trinity as daughter of the Father, mother of the Son, and spouse of the Holy Spirit. She was 'full of grace', not only for being chosen to be God's mother but in her total openness to be filled with that love of God.
- We too are constantly 'graced' and can live out of this grace more fully by opening to the call of God as it unfolds in the unique circumstances of our own lives each day.

Monday 2 January
John 1:19–28

'This is the testimony given by John when the Jews sent priests and Levites from Jerusalem to ask him, 'Who are you?' He confessed and did not deny it, but confessed, 'I am not the Messiah.' And they asked him, 'What then? Are you Elijah?' He said, 'I am not.' 'Are you the prophet?' He answered, 'No.' Then they said to him, 'Who are you? Let us have an answer for those who sent us. What do you say about yourself?' He said,

'I am the voice of one crying out in the wilderness,
"Make straight the way of the Lord",'

as the prophet Isaiah said.

Now they had been sent from the Pharisees. They asked him, 'Why then are you baptising if you are neither the Messiah, nor Elijah, nor the prophet?' John answered them, 'I baptise with water. Among you stands one whom you do not know, the one who is coming after me; I am not worthy to untie the thong of his sandal.' This took place in Bethany across the Jordan where John was baptising.

- In the gospel John the Baptist deflects attention from himself onto Christ. John's role is to 'make straight the way of the Lord' and then to step aside. John represents what all Christians are called to be: witnesses to Christ, heralds of the Good News. Do you see yourself as a witness and a herald?

Tuesday 3 January
John 1:29–34

The next day he saw Jesus coming towards him and declared, 'Here is the Lamb of God who takes away the sin of the world! This is he of whom I said, "After me comes a man who ranks ahead of me because he was before me." I myself did not know him; but I came baptising with water for this reason, that he might be revealed to Israel.' And John testified, 'I saw the Spirit descending from heaven like a dove, and it remained on him. I myself did not know him, but the one who sent me to baptise with water said to me, "He on whom you see the Spirit descend and remain is the one who baptises with the Holy Spirit." And I myself have seen and have testified that this is the Son of God.'

- 'I saw the spirit descending from heaven.' Each one of us has also received the same Spirit in our baptism. It was that Spirit which inspired Jesus in all his work. May the same Spirit inspire us to follow in Jesus' footsteps and join with him in his work to build the Kingdom.

Wednesday 4 January
John 1:35–42

The next day John again was standing with two of his disciples, and as he watched Jesus walk by, he exclaimed, 'Look, here is the Lamb of God!' The two disciples heard him say this, and they followed Jesus. When Jesus turned and saw them following, he said to them, 'What are you looking for?' They said to him, 'Rabbi' (which translated means Teacher), 'where are you staying?' He said to them, 'Come and see.' They came and saw where he was staying, and they remained with him that day. It was about four o'clock in the afternoon. One of the two who heard John speak and followed him was Andrew, Simon Peter's brother. He first found his brother Simon and said to him, 'We have found the Messiah' (which is translated Anointed). He brought Simon to Jesus, who looked at him and said, 'You are Simon son of John. You are to be called Cephas' (which is translated Peter).

- The author of a play takes great care with the first words spoken by the main protagonist. These words must grab our attention and they usually reveal something of that person's character. Here we read the first words spoken by Jesus in the Gospel of John. They are not a teaching, a precept or a challenge (as we might expect), but a simple question: 'What are you looking for?', or 'What do you want?' Jesus asks about our desires so that he can respond to them.

Thursday 5 January
John 1:43–51
The next day Jesus decided to go to Galilee. He found

Philip and said to him, 'Follow me.' Now Philip was from Bethsaida, the city of Andrew and Peter. Philip found Nathanael and said to him, 'We have found him about whom Moses in the law and also the prophets wrote, Jesus son of Joseph from Nazareth.' Nathanael said to him, 'Can anything good come out of Nazareth?' Philip said to him, 'Come and see.' When Jesus saw Nathanael coming towards him, he said of him, 'Here is truly an Israelite in whom there is no deceit!' Nathanael asked him, 'Where did you come to know me?' Jesus answered, 'I saw you under the fig tree before Philip called you.' Nathanael replied, 'Rabbi, you are the Son of God! You are the King of Israel!' Jesus answered, 'Do you believe because I told you that I saw you under the fig tree? You will see greater things than these.' And he said to him, 'Very truly, I tell you, you will see heaven opened and the angels of God ascending and descending upon the Son of Man.'

- The Lord communicates with us in many ways. Sometimes it may seem direct and unambiguous, at other times more indirect, as when the call is mediated by other people. Can you name men and women in your life who brought you to Jesus (as Philip brought Nathanael), or who made you aware of what Jesus was asking of you? Have you been grateful for these mediators?

Friday 6 January
The Epiphany of the Lord (Irl)
Mark 1:7–11

John proclaimed, 'The one who is more powerful than I is coming after me; I am not worthy to stoop down and untie the thong of his sandals. I have baptised you with water; but he will baptise you with the Holy Spirit.'

In those days Jesus came from Nazareth of Galilee and was baptised by John in the Jordan. And just as he was coming up out of the water, he saw the heavens torn apart and the Spirit descending like a dove on him. And a voice came from heaven, 'You are my Son, the Beloved; with you I am well pleased.'

- Imagine yourself witnessing the scene, perhaps standing in the shallows, the water flowing around your ankles. Picture the scene and allow it to unfold. What is it like? The young man from Nazareth joins the queue waiting for John's baptism: a symbol of purifying but also of birth – coming up out of the waters of the womb into a new life as God's beloved child.

- Lord, when I realise that you love me, and are well pleased with me, it is like the start of a new life. As I hear your voice, I know that I have a purpose and a destiny.

Saturday 7 January
John 2:1–11

On the third day there was a wedding in Cana of Galilee, and the mother of Jesus was there. Jesus and his disciples had also been invited to the wedding. When the wine gave out, the mother of Jesus said to him, 'They have no wine.' And Jesus said to her, 'Woman, what concern is that to you and to me? My hour has not yet come.' His mother said to the servants, 'Do whatever he tells you.' Now standing there were six stone water-jars for the Jewish rites of purification, each holding twenty or thirty gallons. Jesus said to them, 'Fill the jars with water.' And they filled them up to the brim. He said to them, 'Now draw some out, and take it to the chief steward.' So they took it. When the steward tasted the water that had become wine, and did not know where it came from (though the servants who had drawn the water knew), the steward called the bridegroom and said to him, 'Everyone serves the good wine first, and then the inferior wine after the guests have become drunk. But you have kept the good wine until now.' Jesus did this, the first of his signs, in Cana of Galilee, and revealed his glory; and his disciples believed in him.

• It is through the Christian community that Jesus comes to us. It is through the Church, through our brothers and sisters in the community, that we learn about the life that God in Jesus wants us to enjoy and share with him and others we meet.

An Advent Retreat

Adapted from Reflections Written by Paul Pace SJ

A time of retreat offers us many chances: a chance to take a step back from the routine and concerns of our everyday lives; a chance to reflect prayerfully on who and what is really important in our lives; a chance to look with honesty at the relationships in our lives and our relationship with creation, and, especially, to focus on our relationship with God; a chance to ask the question 'do these relationships need more nurturing?'

Here is the perfect opportunity to spend some time in the presence of a loving God who is waiting to welcome you, nurture you and draw you into deeper relationship.

Welcome to this year's Advent Retreat. The theme of our retreat this year is Stepping Beyond, and will be inspired by Pope Francis's Encyclical Letter *Fratelli Tutti*, on fraternity and social friendship.

Other words for fraternity include fellowship, friendship and companionship, all of which are central to the Christian message, especially at Christmas. The weeks of Advent are a call to a deeper reflection on the life of Jesus as he stepped beyond his world into ours as our companion and friend. Advent is a time to help us prepare to welcome Jesus our Saviour, God made man in Bethlehem.

In *Fratelli Tutti* Pope Francis draws inspiration from the example of St Francis of Assisi, whose life involved walking 'alongside the poor, the abandoned, the sick, the discarded, the last' (*FT*, 2). These most vulnerable must be central and Pope Francis shares how Francis of Assisi demonstrated a 'heart without boundaries, capable of going beyond the distances due to origin, nationality, colour or religion' (*FT*, 3), open to foreigners.

Pope Francis is inviting us to do the same. Let us step beyond our usual spaces, let us imagine a world where we are all brothers and sisters, friends even, and let us commit ourselves to bringing it closer.

Many of us will feel that we have tried this often enough, and the world is not getting any better. Very often it seems to be getting even worse, where the leaders we choose encourage us to think only of ourselves and of our country, of those who are exactly like us. We happily profess and praise equality as one of the biggest conquests of our times, but we must admit we are living in a world of increasing inequality, in all senses: the rich become richer and have better access to health services, while the poor are expected to remain resigned to their unfortunate lot. Migration is the magic card so cynically used to win votes, so that we just turn a blind eye to atrocities committed to enable us to retain our privileged status: we close not only our borders but also our hearts.

The changes needed are so big, so it seems reasonable to just give up and live within our small world as best we can. Yet Advent promises us a Saviour, who by stepping out of his world into ours, is someone who shows us that this is not so difficult to achieve. Not a wonder worker who will put the world to rights without demanding anything, Jesus is rather a true saviour who, in sharing our human condition, inspires and empowers us to work towards a better world.

Over these weeks of Advent, we will look at some of the themes and reflections found in *Fratelli Tutti* as a guide to living Advent more fully. In writing this encyclical Pope Francis is hoping 'that in the face of present day attempts to eliminate or ignore others, we may prove capable of responding with a new vision of fraternity and social friendship that will not remain at the level of words' (*FT*, 6).

The many people we meet during these weeks of Advent – John the Baptist, Mary, the Shepherds and Wise Men and so on – were invited to step beyond themselves into a new way and embrace a new vision.

Their openness to recognising the signs and accepting this invitation allowed the kingdom of God to come among us through the person of Jesus. Let us pray this Advent that we too can see the signs and hear God's call for a greater fulfilment of the Word made Flesh in our own lives, in our world, for all our brothers and sisters.

Practicalities

We start with some practical hints that might help you if you haven't made a retreat like this before, or will act as reminders if you have. You might like to consider these headings: how, where, when and what. One question to consider as a 'how', is how long you feel that you can devote to each session of the retreat. It's good to decide this in advance and try to stick to it. Don't give up too soon if the prayer seems a little dull or continue too long if it seems to be going well. Each of the retreat sessions should take about 20–25 minutes. Just choose a time that you can comfortably fit into your routine, having spent a few minutes preparing yourself and perhaps some more time afterwards noting in writing, in pictures or in whatever way you choose what the key points of invitation or resistance were for you. Whatever your responses and reactions, keep a brief note, as a pattern may emerge that proves a helpful guide when you look back.

Under the headings 'where' and 'when', you might like to give some thought to what time of day is best for you to pray – morning, evening, or in the middle of the day? This might also suggest another question: Where will you find it easiest to pray and reflect in this way?

Finally, under the heading of 'what', ask yourself what you are making this retreat for. What are the gifts and graces you would hope to receive from God during these times of prayer? Make sure that you start the prayer by asking God for these gifts and graces and try to be open to whatever else God wants to give you. Often we do not know what we really need!

When you have taken a while to consider these questions, you'll be ready to begin this prayerful time of reflecting on 'stepping beyond'. Before you start, take a moment to become aware of God's welcoming gaze of love on you as you meet him in this way. Become aware also of all those others around the world who are praying this retreat alongside you and know that you are part of this worldwide community of prayer.

Throughout this retreat we will make reference to the encyclical *Fratelli Tutti*. Please feel free to explore the document further, for more clarification or reflection.

SESSION 1

Stepping Beyond – From Mere Neighbours to Brothers and Sisters

Invitation to stillness

Begin by paying attention to your breathing, without changing the rhythm … Notice your breathing in … and your breathing out … the rhythm … the depth … the feel of the air entering and leaving your mouth or nose … take three deeper breaths …

Reading

Isaiah 11:1–9

A shoot shall come out from the stock of Jesse,
and a branch shall grow out of his roots.
The spirit of the Lord shall rest on him,
the spirit of wisdom and understanding,
the spirit of counsel and might,
the spirit of knowledge and the fear of the Lord.
His delight shall be in the fear of the Lord.

He shall not judge by what his eyes see,
 or decide by what his ears hear;
but with righteousness he shall judge the poor,
and decide with equity for the meek of the earth;
he shall strike the earth with the rod of his
    mouth,

and with the breath of his lips he shall kill the
    wicked.
Righteousness shall be the belt around his waist,
and faithfulness the belt around his loins.

The wolf shall live with the lamb,
the leopard shall lie down with the kid,
the calf and the lion and the fatling together,
and a little child shall lead them.
The cow and the bear shall graze,
their young shall lie down together;
and the lion shall eat straw like the ox.
The nursing child shall play over the hole of the
    asp,
and the weaned child shall put its hand on the
    adder's den.
They will not hurt or destroy
on all my holy mountain;
for the earth will be full of the knowledge of the
    Lord
as the waters cover the sea.

Reflect

In these first days of Advent, the liturgy reminds us of
the promises regarding the Messiah and his time. It
will be a time that brings together all peoples of the
earth around the same table, where even the animals
that are usually hostile can live in harmony. After

listening to Isaiah's account of the Peaceful Kingdom we will consider in this first of our reflections on *Fratelli Tutti* how we might live in this same harmony as brothers and sisters.

In the words of Benedict XVI we are told 'as society becomes ever more globalised, it makes us neighbours, but does not make us brothers and sisters'. These wise words from his encyclical on love and truth still ring true, and this paradox is what moved Pope Francis to write his own encyclical on universal brotherhood and sisterhood.

Inspired once more by the Saint of Assisi, Pope Francis invites us to a life 'marked by the flavour of the Gospel … in his simple and direct way, Saint Francis expressed the essence of a fraternal openness that allows us to acknowledge, appreciate and love each person, regardless of physical proximity, regardless of where he or she was born or lives' (*FT*, 1).

Unfortunately, in our world this ideal of belonging to a single human family is fading. On the contrary, while equality is enshrined in solemn documents that claim to fashion our relationships, in practice we are encouraged to stress our differences rather than what we share. For our politicians the best way to gain power lies not in proposing a project of wide vision and fraternity but in cynically inviting us to a life of isolation, behind high walls that keep others away, 'thinking that we are all-powerful, while failing to realise that we are all in the same boat' (*FT*, 30).

However, as our reading for today tells us, we are invited to create a world where 'the wolf shall live with the lamb, the leopard shall lie down with the kid, the calf and the lion and the fatling together, and a little child shall lead them. They will not hurt or destroy all my holy mountain; for the earth will be full of the knowledge of the Lord' (Isaiah 11:6,8).

'Isolation and withdrawal into one's own interests are never the way to restore hope and bring about renewal. Isolation – no; closeness – yes. Culture clash no; culture of encounter – yes' (*FT*, 30).

Talk to God

As you listened to the peaceful kingdom scripture, was there a phrase, a particular animal pairing that stayed with you? Stay with this image and talk to God about what it means to you and your ideas about peace ...

What arises in you when you compare our current human family and the peaceful kingdom? A longing for more? A sadness for how things are? Or perhaps a sense of hope or joy at the commonality you find around you? Sit with the Lord now, in whatever you are feeling about this ...

You might like to spend these final moments talking to God as one friend speaks to another about your hope for human harmony. Notice if God stirs within you a possible action or response to help move this hope into a reality ...

SESSION 2

Stepping Beyond Ourselves to Those Who Suffer

Invitation to Stillness

Call to mind any concerns you have been carrying recently … as you breathe out, share them with God … you might even be able to hand some of these over, at least for now … as you breathe out, hand them over to God … each time you breathe in, breathe in God's love for you … let it fill your body … take three deeper breaths, keeping this up …

Reading

Isaiah 40:3–5

A voice cries out:

> 'In the wilderness prepare the way of the Lord,
> Make straight in the desert a highway for our
>   God.
> Every valley shall be lifted up, and every
>   mountain and hill be made low;
> The uneven ground shall become level, and the
>   rough places a plain.
> Then the glory of the Lord shall be revealed, and
>   all people shall see it together,
> For the mouth of the Lord has spoken.'

Reflect

John the Baptist, whom we meet during these weeks of Advent, was a prophetic figure. A prophet is someone who speaks the truth and challenges us to shake out of our usual ways of seeing and doing things. John's message was uncomfortable for many at the time and perhaps is still uncomfortable for us today. It calls us to step beyond ourselves to a place of community where there is justice and care for all our brothers and sisters who suffer and when we do this 'then the glory of the Lord shall be revealed and all people shall see it together'.

In keeping with this theme of caring for those who suffer, Pope Francis in *Fratelli Tutti* (Chapter 2) uses the powerful parable of the Good Samaritan (Luke 10:25–37). This parable deals with a problem we already meet in the first pages of the Bible. God asks Cain: 'Where is your brother Abel?' Cain's answer is one that we ourselves give all too often: 'Am I my brother's keeper?' (Genesis 4:9). We often look for answers that justify our inaction and indifference towards the immense suffering that surrounds us. One way of doing that is to form closed groups where we only care for those who are like us, excluding all others. However, listening to the message from John the Baptist, we are called to make 'the uneven ground … level, and the rough places a plain'.

In the parable of the Good Samaritan 'only one

person stopped, approached the man, and cared for him personally, even spending his own money to provide for his needs. He also gave him something that in our frenetic world we cling to tightly: he gave him his time. Certainly, he had his own plans for that day, his own needs, commitments and desires. Yet he was able to put all that aside when confronted with someone in need. Without even knowing the injured man, he saw him as deserving of his time and attention' (*FT*, 63).

The Pope applies this parable not only to relationships between individuals, but also to the way we organise our societies: Do our societies include or exclude? If we live like neighbours, our societies will know how to identify with the vulnerabilities in their midst, lifting up and rehabilitating the fallen for the sake of the common good. 'At the same time, [the parable] warns us about the attitude of those who think only of themselves and fail to shoulder the inevitable responsibilities of life as it is.' (*FT*, 67).

Pope Francis insists that 'the decision to include or exclude those lying wounded along the roadside can serve as a criterion for judging every economic, political, social and religious project. Each day we have to decide whether to be Good Samaritans or indifferent bystanders' (*FT*, 69).

During Advent we prepare ourselves for the coming of the true Good Samaritan, Jesus Christ, who takes pity on our situation and comes to pick us up and heal us. He then tells us, 'Go and do likewise' (Luke 10:37).

Talk to God

As you begin to talk to God now, turn your attention to Christ's life for a moment ... a baby born in a simple manger; born into a suffering world ... a life lived in service of the suffering, before suffering for us on a cross. Spend some time sitting now with Jesus, who has experienced the very depths of suffering ... Who is suffering and in your heart today? Talk to God about them now ...

In these closing moments, you might like to ask God for a clear sense of how you can help those suffering around you ... noticing where you feel stirred to act ...

SESSION 3

Stepping Beyond Our Borders – Welcoming the Stranger

Invitation to stillness

Notice what is on your mind ... let each thought that comes gently drop away ... notice how you are feeling at this moment ... can you put a name on a feeling? ... can you locate where in your body you are feeling this? ... notice how you are in your body today ... relaxed or tense ... cold or warm ... tired or wide awake ... how is your body? ... however you are, let God look at you with love and welcome you to this time together ...

Reading

Matthew 2:13–15

Now after they had left, an angel of the Lord appeared to Joseph in a dream and said, 'Get up, take the child and his mother, and flee to Egypt, and remain there until I tell you; for Herod is about to search for the child, to destroy him.' Then Joseph got up, took the child and his mother by night, and went to Egypt, and remained there until the death of Herod. This was to fulfil what had been spoken by the Lord through the prophet, 'Out of Egypt I have called my son.'

Reflect

On Christmas Day we celebrate Jesus, who was born away from his town, among people he did not know; there was not even a place for him at the inn. As we reflect on the reading from St Matthew we hear that shortly after his birth, Jesus had to flee for his life with Mary and Joseph and lived his childhood years in a foreign country, speaking a language that was not his own, among people who professed a different religion.

In this week's reflection, as we consider the flight

of the Holy Family, we are being invited to step beyond our borders and to welcome the stranger. As we continue to reflect on the message of *Fratelli Tutti* we are reminded that we live in a world where the issue of migration is presented as a basic issue in politics. Many leaders profess that the solution to migration lies simply in keeping migrants out of the country by any means. It is no surprise that the problem only gets bigger, as the world becomes colder and ready to accept measures that it would find totally unacceptable in other areas.

In one of his most famous phrases, the Pope called this 'the globalisation of indifference'. It is no wonder the issue of migration and the welcome of refugees has a prominent place in *Fratelli Tutti*'s invitation to step beyond. During this season of Advent, when we see the many images of migrants and hear the media reports of their plight, do we ever consider the similarities of Jesus, Mary and Joseph, as the angel told Joseph to 'Get up, take the child and his mother and flee to Egypt'?

In *Fratelli Tutti* Pope Francis tells us that we should strive to treat migrants and refugees with love and compassion. 'Our response to the arrival of migrating persons can be summarised by four words: welcome, protect, promote and integrate' (*FT*, 29). He continues, 'No one will ever openly deny that [migrants and refugees] are human beings, yet in practice, by our decisions and the way we treat them, we can show that we consider them less worthy, less important, less human. For Christians, this way of thinking and acting is unacceptable' (*FT*, 39). In these weeks of Advent we pray: Come Lord Jesus, open our hearts that we may not be indifferent to the needs of our brothers and sisters, but, with much love, strive to step beyond our comfort zones to welcome, protect, promote and integrate them.

Talk to God

What has struck you during your reflection time today? Perhaps a particular image of refugees has stayed in your mind? Or perhaps you can picture the scene of the Holy Family in your imagination … what they were wearing … the way they moved and travelled … their gestures and emotions? Reflect on these things with God now.

What stirs in you when you think about stepping beyond to help the stranger? This might be something you are unfamiliar with, or something you are seeking to do at the moment … Talk to God about where you are in this.

In these closing moments, you might like to thank God for all the strangers who have entered your life. Ask God to reveal someone HE might like you to reach out to today …

SESSION 4

Stepping Beyond – A Journey of Peace among Religions

Invitation to stillness

Begin by paying attention to your breathing, without changing the rhythm ... Notice your breathing in ... and your breathing out ... the rhythm ... the depth ... the feel of the air entering and leaving your mouth or nose ... take three deeper breaths ...

Reading

Luke 2:8–14

In that region there were shepherds living in the fields, keeping watch over their flock by night. Then an angel of the Lord stood before them, and the glory of the Lord shone around them, and they were terrified. But the angel said to them, 'Do not be afraid, for see – I am bringing you good news of great joy for all the people: to you is born this day in the city of David a Saviour, who is the Messiah, the Lord. This will be a sign for you: you will find a child wrapped in bands of cloth and lying in a manger.' And suddenly there was with the angel a multitude of the heavenly host, praising God and saying, 'Glory to God in the highest heaven, and on earth peace among those whom he favours!'

Reflect

As we continue our journey through Advent, *Fratelli Tutti* continues to offer us much wisdom and, perhaps, challenges. In listening to this beautiful reading, we recall that on Christmas night the angels proclaimed a message of good news to the shepherds and of peace to all those of good will. What is striking about this reading is that this message was proclaimed to all, not only to those of a particular religion. God chose the wise men from the East to bring the news to Jerusalem that the King of the Jews was born. Have you ever considered what the world would be like if all religions everywhere were to come together and work for the recognition of every person's dignity? What a huge impact we would have!

Pope Francis tells us that, ultimately, the real foundation that we are all brothers and sisters lies in our belief that we are all children of the same Father. 'A journey of peace is possible between religions. Its point of departure must be God's way of seeing things. God does not see with his eyes, God sees with his heart, and God's love is the same for everyone, regardless of religion. Even if they are atheists, his love is the same' (*FT*, 281).

It follows 'that we believers need to find occasions to speak with one another and to act together for the common good and the promotion of the poor' (*FT*, 282). During these weeks of Advent can we find these occasions in our daily lives?

This has nothing to do with watering down or concealing our deepest convictions when we encounter others who think differently from us. We can only reach out to others when we are sure of our identity and our beliefs.

Pope Francis tells us that 'the Church esteems the ways in which God works in other religions, and rejects nothing of what is true and holy in these religions. She has a high regard for their manner of life and conduct, their precepts and doctrines' (*FT*, 277). Our lives often bring us in contact with others of different religions. Yet we Christians are very much aware that 'if the music of the Gospel ceases to resonate in our very being, we will lose the joy born of compassion, the tender love born of trust, the capacity for reconciliation that has its source in our knowledge that we have been forgiven and sent forth' (*FT*, 277).

Let us not lose the music of the Gospel as we prepare for Christmas. If you try to reach out, step beyond, offer an encounter of fraternity, friendship and companionship this Christmas season, you might be surprised at how much we all have in common! Let us remember the words of the angel: 'Do not be afraid! For behold, I bring you good news of great joy that will be for all the people.'

Talk to God

Take a moment to reflect on your own response to people of other religions, or those who think differently from you. How have you been challenged or stirred by today's session?

'Do not be afraid; for see – I am bringing you good news of great joy for all the people'. Are you aware of the good news of great joy that you have been given to carry and share with others? You might like to ask God for a renewed sense of this joy in your life today …

How might you be called to share the 'music of the Gospel' this Christmas and beyond? In these closing moments, you might like to ask the Holy Spirit to open your eyes to a new sense of calling in this way …

SESSION 5

Stepping Beyond the Crib into Today's Messy World

Invitation to Stillness

Using a mantra can help us to find stillness in the busyness of our lives. Take a few moments to settle yourself into this time of prayer. Notice where you are, how you are, what is going on for you. Give it all to God, then ask for what you seek in this prayer.

It might be to know Jesus more as Lord or Messiah or friend, or just more intimately. Take the Aramaic word 'Marantha', which means 'come, O Lord', and repeat it as you breathe. Marantha. Repeat the word for a couple of minutes and, if you become distracted, simply return to the word.

Reading

Luke 2: 15–20

When the angels had left them and gone into heaven, the shepherds said to one another, 'Let us go now to Bethlehem and see this thing that has taken place, which the Lord has made known to us.' So they went with haste and found Mary and Joseph, and the child lying in the manger. When they saw this, they made known what had been told to them about this child; and all who heard it were amazed at what the shepherds told them. But Mary treasured all these words and pondered them in her heart. The shepherds returned, glorifying and praising God for all they had heard and seen, as it had been told them.

Reflect

'Let us go now to Bethlehem and see this thing that has taken place.' What better way to pray, than taking some time to look at the scene of the birth of Jesus and to go to Bethlehem? Take the image on a Christmas card, or spend time before the crib you have in your house or in your church, or look for a nativity scene on the Internet. What is it like to 'go now to Bethlehem'?

What strikes me most when I look at the scene of the nativity? Above all the persons, Jesus, just born, looking like every other newborn, beautiful but so tiny, totally dependent on others. Mary, his mother, like every other mother who has just given birth, tired yet unimaginably happy. Joseph, full of wonder at what has just happened, so happy to be doing what he was asked to do by the angel. The shepherds, simple, poor people, still amazed at the vision of the angels and the news that they had just heard. Everyone in this crib scene was called to step beyond their own ways, their own road, and their ways of thinking for the greater glory of God. How was this possible? They were open to the way of love and trusted in the one who guided them.

I put myself in the poor stable. I can feel the joy and love, the deep peace, the wonder, but also the utter poverty, the darkness, the strangeness, the smell of animals and wet hay. Moreover, this Saviour, the one who fulfils God's promises, is born in great poverty, outside of his own town, not even in a home or an inn, but in a stable for animals. How does this impact on me today?

We remember the words of the angel 'Do not be afraid; for see – I am bringing you good news of great joy for all the people: to you is born this day in the city of David a Saviour, who is the Messiah, the Lord.'

Many parts of our world are in a real mess now. It often looks and feels and smells like the stable of Bethlehem. Some parts of my life may be messy too. I stay with a word or image that strikes me most, as I ask myself whether the birth of Jesus is for me good news of great joy. I reflect on the fact that I have been given a Saviour, one who makes up for my shortcomings and those of the world.

Prayer

An Ecumenical Christian Prayer

O God, Trinity of love,
from the profound communion of your divine
    life,
pour out upon us a torrent of fraternal love.
Grant us the love reflected in the actions of
    Jesus,
in his family of Nazareth,
and in the early Christian community.

Grant that we Christians may live the Gospel,
discovering Christ in each human being,
recognising him crucified
in the sufferings of the abandoned
and forgotten of our world,

and risen in each brother or sister
who makes a new start.

Come, Holy Spirit, show us your beauty,
reflected in all the peoples of the earth,
so that we may discover anew
that all are important and all are necessary,
different faces of the one humanity
that God so loves. Amen.

Conclusion

As we conclude our reflections on *Fratelli Tutti* we are reminded that after their encounter at the stable in Bethlehem 'the shepherds returned, glorifying and praising God for all they had heard and seen, as it had been told to them'. The shepherds were stepping beyond the crib at Bethlehem into today's messy world. We are called to do the same by reaching out in fraternity and social fellowship to all our brothers and sisters we meet as we return along the road.

Pope Francis invites us to remember that 'human beings are so made that they cannot live, develop and find fulfilment except in the sincere gift of self to others. No one can experience the true beauty of life without relating to others, without having real faces to love' (*FT*, 87). 'Love also impels us towards universal communion. No one can mature or find fulfilment by withdrawing from others. By its very nature, love calls for growth in openness and the ability to accept others' (*FT*, 95).

Over these weeks of Advent we have been invited to listen to the words of Pope Francis as he encourages us to walk 'alongside the poor, the abandoned, the sick, the discarded, the last'. We have been encouraged to step beyond ourselves, and in following the example of St Francis of Assisi to have a 'heart without boundaries, capable of going beyond the distances due to origin, nationality, colour or religion, open to foreigners', open to all (*FT*, 3).

We have been accompanied on this journey by many key people in the Advent story. They were also called to move out of their comfort zones and to step beyond themselves in embracing a new way, one which ultimately brought them to the humble stable where the birth of a child brought the fulfilment of salvation for all people. They continue to walk with us now as we open our hearts and reach out in love to our brothers and sisters. O Come, O Come, Emmanuel, God is with us.